EDWARD SACKVILLE-WEST

GRAHAM SUTHERLAND

PENGUIN BOOKS

THE PENGUIN MODERN PAINTERS

Editor Sir Kenneth Clark

Made and Printed in Great Britain by Hunt, Barnard & Company, Ltd.
The Sign of the Dolphin, London and Aylesbury, Buckinghamshire
Colour Plates by W. F. Sedgwick, Ltd.

Published by
Penguin Books Limited
Harmondsworth, Middlesex, England
1943

COLOUR PLATES

BLACK AND WHITE PLATES

Plate 2   PASTORAL (1930), $7\frac{1}{2} \times 5$, *etching*; owned by Edward Sackville-West, Esq.

Plate 4   ROAD WITH ROCKS (1936), $22 \times 13\frac{1}{2}$, *pen and wash*; owned by Sir Kenneth Clark
     Exhibited 1940 London National Gallery. Some drawings of past 50 years. Temple Newsam 1941

Plate 6   TREE TRUNK SPRAWLING (1938), $18\frac{3}{4} \times 25$, *oil*; owned by Artist
     Exhibited Rosenberg & Helft Ltd., 1938

Plate 8   BLACK LANDSCAPE (1937), $31\frac{1}{2} \times 18\frac{1}{4}$, *water-colour*; owned by Sir Kenneth Clark
     Exhibited Rosenberg & Helft 1938

Plate 10   ASSOCIATION OF OAKS (1940), 19×27, *gouache*; owned by F. Bravington, Esq.
     Exhibited Leicester Galleries 1940

Plate 12   PRECIPITOUS ROAD TO HILLS (1940), $26\frac{1}{2} \times 18$, *gouache*; owned by Raymond Mortimer, Esq.
     Exhibited Leicester Galleries 1940. Temple Newsam 1941

Plate 14   FALLEN TREE WITH SUNSET (1940), $20 \times 26\frac{1}{2}$, *oil*; owned by Contemporary Art Society
     Exhibited Leicester Gallery 1940. Temple Newsam, Leeds 1941

Plate 16   LANDSCAPE WITH LOW CLIFF AND WOODS (1938), $31\frac{1}{2} \times 18\frac{1}{4}$, *water-colour*; owned by C. Anderson, Esq.
     Exhibited Rosenberg & Helft Ltd. 1938. Temple Newsam, Leeds 1941

Plate 18   DEVASTATION 1941—City—Burnt-out Interior (1941), $21\frac{1}{2} \times 31\frac{1}{2}$, *ink, chalk, and wash*;
                                             owned by War Artists Committee

Plate 20   WESTERN HILLS, 36×22, *oil*; owned by Edward Sackville-West, Esq.
     First painted 1938 and exhibited at Rosenberg & Helft Ltd. under title of "Hills", reworked 1941 and exhibited at Redfern Gallery

Plate 22   BLASTED OAK (1941), 12×15, *pen and wash*; owned by Edward Sackville-West, Esq.
     Exhibited Leicester Galleries 1941

Plate 24   DEVASTATION 1941—East End—Burnt-out Paper Rolls (1941), $18\frac{1}{4} \times 12\frac{7}{8}$, *ink, chalk and wash*;
                                             owned by War Artists Committee

Plate 26   DARK HILL (1940), $26\frac{1}{2} \times 18\frac{1}{2}$, *water-colour*; owned by Hiram Winterbotham, Esq.

Plate 28   TREE FORM (1941), $12 \times 15\frac{1}{2}$, *oil*; owned by Temple Newsam, Leeds

Plate 30   FOLDED HILLS (1943), 15×11, *pen and wash*; *study for painting in oil*; owned by Artist

Plate 32   TREE FORMS (1943), $20\frac{1}{2} \times 27$, *ink, chalk and gouache*; owned by Artist

GRAHAM SUTHERLAND

GRAHAM SUTHERLAND was born in London on August 24th, 1903. The first nine years of his life were spent at Merton Park, Surrey, and at Rustington, in Sussex. In 1912 he went to boarding school at Sutton; and it is from this time, during some holidays spent at Swanage, that he himself dates that mysterious intimacy with Nature which has since developed into the basis of his art—its *raison d'être*. I say "mysterious" advisedly, for there is nothing so occult, so removed from usual understanding, as the interaction of two planes of life: the human being on the one hand, on the other all that vast theory of organisms, from stones to trees, in which the characteristic movement of life is not adjusted to our vision; so that we can only *feel* it, if we be exceptionally sensitive, or perceive it at most in that immobility—ominous or serene or merely intense—which is like that of the gyroscope a-spin. In childhood this experience of "inanimate objects" as living with a life that is both like and unlike our own, is common to all of us, because the younger the human being the less distinct are the senses one from another, so that what is perceived at all tends to be experienced by the whole body at once. But in adults the faculty of retaining this valuable intuition of Essence is the prerogative of artists, though not all of them care to use it. In Graham Sutherland, however, the experience was too constant and too vivid to be obliterated: the luscious pastures and leafage in the neighbourhood of Rustington, the whites and silver greens of the country behind Swanage, stepped down out of the background, so to speak, and offered themselves to a pair of eyes that were henceforward to act as a powerful magnifying glass to every grass and leaf, every wrinkle in an old tree-stump.

These years were fairly happy ones, for the boy had an aptitude and liking for Latin and Greek, which the school taught particularly well. But in 1914 he was sent to Epsom College, where the educational bias was scientific rather than classical, and where in consequence, for the next four years, he was acutely miserable. But the pressure of discontent forced to the surface the experiences he had accumulated in Sussex and Dorset: he began to draw, but for himself alone, without tuition or encouragement. In 1918, having matriculated in Classics, he was apprenticed as an engineer in the Midland Railway works at Derby, and remained there a year. This experience, irksome as it may have seemed at the time, cannot, I think, be regarded as so much waste of time where Sutherland is concerned, for it evidently accustomed his hand to a linear exactitude which—all appearances to the contrary—in fact supplies the fundamental structure of all his mature painting. Examine *Boulder*, or *Western Hills*, or *Red Landscape*, and you will observe that a discreet but tough thread of black cotton stitches the design as it were a coat—sometimes above the paint, at others running below it to reappear in some passage further on. I use the image of a thread to establish the fact that Sutherland uses line to bind together, rather than divide, though it is significant that in his very latest works, the portraits of tin miners, the technique is as dis-

junctive as Holbein's. The point will be reverted to later; here it is only necessary to emphasize the importance of his work as an apprentice-engineer in determining the method of his art.

After a year spent in this fashion it became clear to Sutherland that he was not cut out for engineering; so he left Derby and at last set to work in earnest to become a painter. The first step in this direction was Goldsmith's School of Art, an affiliation of London University at New Cross, where he remained from 1919 to 1925. Here he started on his fourteen-year career as an etcher, making frequent expeditions to Arundel and the neighbourhood, to draw from nature and renew the æsthetic experience of his childhood. In 1925 his etchings began to sell; and as at this time it became necessary for him to earn a livelihood, he left New Cross and set up on his own, in London itself, at the same time teaching in an evening class at Kingston. One thing leads to another: Sutherland's reputation as an etcher grew, and in 1927 he was engaged to teach that anxious craft at the Chelsea School of Art. These were the years of the etching boom, which came to an abrupt end in 1930; but Sutherland continued to teach in the Chelsea school until the outbreak of war.

Here it seems fitting to mention that it was at Goldsmith's School that Sutherland met the girl who, in 1929, became his wife and who, through her single-minded devotion and her sympathetic understanding of her husband's art, has been the greatest human inspiration and encouragement of his career.

It may have been a coincidence that he should have taken up etching after his year in the railway workshops; it looks, however, like a result. In any case, though his etchings show his preference for well-furnished spaces (a preference since maintained: his management of bare shapes is noticeably less happy), the passages of darkest shadow are still made of that same black thread, rolled into a mass and pulled out again to define, with an exquisite virtuosity derived from Samuel Palmer, the centres of visual interest.

Between 1930 and 1934 Sutherland made a tentative sortie in the London Group. But the pictures he painted and exhibited during this period represent an abortive attempt at an individual style, rather than anything that could be called an "early manner". If it is permissible to use that term at all in Sutherland's case, it must refer rather to such etchings as the *Pastoral* (1930), in which the oak-tree on the right displays clearly some elements of his mature vision and method.

To teach a subject is one of the best ways of learning it. In 1935 Sutherland began to teach Composition and Book Illustration at the Chelsea School. At the same time he received commissions for posters from the Shell Company, the Orient Line, and London Transport. These activities must be considered together with his later designs for fabrics, papers and china, since all of them display exquisite taste and decorative talent of a high order—features with which, in his pictures, he has no particular truck. Indeed, it would be difficult to imagine paintings that have, or are intended to have, less *decorative* value than Graham Sutherland's; and taste, which goes with decoration, is there merely latent in the degree of emphasis.

The division of an artist's *œuvre* into periods is usually inevitable, though always attended by misconceptions and half-truths. In Sutherland's case the assessment up to the present is relatively easy, for he seems to have made fewer false starts than many painters and has always been scrupulous in destroying or concealing what he knew to be failures. In any case he is the most homogeneous of contemporary English painters: his art progresses slowly and *en bloc*. His last etching, made in 1930, gave a signal. What happens in these cases belongs to the arcana of personality; but it is certain that, round about 1936, when Sutherland first visited Pembrokeshire, the accumulated experience of fifteen years' work at last precipitated a style which was to prove a precise and durable instrument of expression.

"It was in this country that I began to learn painting": thus begins a most revealing passage in a letter to Mr. Colin Anderson. He continues: "It seemed impossible here for me to sit down and make finished paintings 'from Nature'. Indeed, there were no ready-made subjects to paint. The spaces and concentrations of this clearly constructed land were stuff for storing in the mind. Their essence was intellectual and emotional, if I may say so. I found that I could express what I felt only by paraphrasing what I saw. Moreover, such country did not seem to make men appear little as does some country of the grander sort. I felt just as much part of the earth as my features were part of me. I did not feel that my imagination was in conflict with the real, but that reality was a dispersed and disintegrated form of imagination."

So complete and far-reaching a statement could only be made by an artist conscious that he knows what he has been about; thus to the following years (1936-40) belong a number of what I take to be Graham Sutherland's most considerable pictures: the *Red Tree* (not here reproduced), the *Rocky Landscape with Cairn*, the *Green Tree Form*, the superb *Black Landscape*, the *Landscape with Low Cliff and Woods*, the *Gorse on Sea-wall*, the *Small Boulder*. Since 1937 he has lived mainly at Trottiscliffe, under the chalky slope of the North Downs, near Maidstone; but the pictures he has painted there have mostly been from sketches made elsewhere, and the characteristic features of the Kentish landscape do not on the whole appear. It would seem, indeed, as if he needed the fresh impact of a place suddenly arrived in, to arrest his eye, for a single year (1939–40) spent in Gloucestershire failed signally to produce anything in which the special features of that county could be said to figure. In no sense a regional painter, he takes his material where he finds it, but only finds it in a few places—countries of adoption such as the wild, stony fields and moors on the Atlantic coasts of Pembrokeshire and Cornwall. That so few kinds of landscape are of any "use" to him gives the measure of his intransigence as an artist, and lies also at the root of his absolute originality.

This originality is the result, no doubt, of a long process of inward, but not of outward, gestation. Graham Sutherland has not shown the public more than two or three phases of the process; but we know enough to trace the sources of his inspiration. It is a road not often travelled, and even now quite unimpeded by traffic, that leads from the later Turner to—not Monet—but Picasso. The reason for this deviation from a usual process is provided by Blake and Samuel Palmer, most obviously perhaps the focus of Sutherland's deepest admiration. The *mystique* of Nature assumes in their inventions a less purely pictorial quality than it does in Turner, who became more and more solely interested in the influence of light on the Thing-as-it-Appears. What Sutherland has learnt from Blake discards the pretentious human anatomy (his recent figure painting follows Raphael rather than late Greek and Roman sculpture), but retains the colour scale imposed by the English climate on the stuff of our island—the egg yellows, the veiled pinks, the sudden blacks. In many of his mature landscapes (the *Black Landscape*, the *Small Boulder*, the *Dark Hill*, the *Cliff Road*, the *Road and Hills in Setting Sun*) it seems that he has painted as it were the "negative" of the proposed scene, so that it is the black passages which proclaim the presence of light, while the yellows, blues and streaks of vermilion and violet become the representatives of night. The result does not placate the eye: in fact, Sutherland's harmonic progressions will seem in general as rugose as Beethoven's, to those accustomed to the blandness of most contemporary English *gammes*. There came a moment, indeed, when, as with Palmer himself, Sutherland's obsession with darkness resulted in a bass octave of so fuliginous an obscurity that some of his finest inventions, such as Sir Kenneth Clark's *Landscape with Sullen Sky*, can only be properly distinguished in very bright daylight and cannot be reproduced satisfactorily at all. "Dark with excess of light", these pictures have a quality unique in modern landscape painting—an expression of doom and foreboding obtained along the same lines by John Piper in his portraits of the great houses of England in the final stage of their decay—or again in the figure compositions of Eugene Berman, where a brooding sadness and dejection, as of a nearly depopulated planet, reaches us through a floating, ghostly line or a congress of deceitful colours that glare with the eye-like brilliance of flowers in twilight.

Blake and Palmer, however, are the pointers to the emotion behind Sutherland's painting, and the second in particular must be held responsible for the "inset", jewel-like impression some of his smallest pictures (e.g. the *Small Boulder*) make, as if the eye were observing large canvases through the wrong end of a telescope. This effect, peculiar to-day and strangely moving, has in it again something of the primitive and proceeds, I think, from the habit of taking literally the reports of a close-up view. But in amassing a vocabulary of adequate images; in the integration of those images in the syntax of composition; in the building up of a system of design that should respond immediately to the emotion evoked by the object: in all these important respects Sutherland has above all obeyed the manifold precept of Picasso. That this is not immediately obvious is due to the fact that the forms with which Sutherland deals, being those of Nature, have not the tooled and polished quality of the *objets d'intérieur* which are the raw material of Picasso's abstractions. Yet the aim is similar, though the process had to be different; for, unlike "made" things, natural forms are essentially picturesque and thus arouse appropriate attention. A street of houses may lull the eye to insensibility—which is why a certain type of stupid person only feels at home in a town. In a landscape the eye is caught into awareness at every turn.

I have used the word "abstraction"—dangerously, for one cannot properly speak of abstract art as one speaks of "pure" mathematics. All art is a commentary on the world of appearances, and—as in music, so also in painting—any sequence of notes can be regarded as a theme unless it is used as figuration. Truly abstract painting would, therefore, be literally invisible, or else tend merely to return to the palette: a development more than adumbrated in Turner's very last canvases. That, however, must be regarded as an eccentricity, leading nowhere; the true aim of abstraction being, I take it, to dissolve objects into invisibility and then to bring them back to the point where they fulfil the requirements of your particular vision. The process can, of course, best be studied in Impressionist painting, where Seurat, for instance, represents a world brought half-way back from the invisible heaven in which, essentially, all objects repose. The technique, which belongs to the mysteries of art, may be imagined after the pattern of a game of billiards, in which the ball is directed at the cushion so as to return, not to the point of the cue that sped it, but to some other exactly intended spot on the table.

Sutherland's task was now (*circa* 1935) to realize in the above fashion that comprehensive and interfusing vision of Nature received for the first time thirty years previously and never lost sight of. Most artists whose devotion is given to line become portrait painters; and Graham Sutherland is, in fact, one, though his portraits are of tree-trunks (e.g. the *Blasted Oak*), of grass-blades, of huge hemlock flowers, of old stones, rather than of human faces or arrangements of books and fruit. But to do this thoroughly meant the renunciation of Perspective in the interests of what was essentially a non-scenic vision of land-scape. This brings us to the centre of our subject. As a glance through the reproductions of his work during the period 1936-40 is enough to show, Sutherland eschewed perspective in the effort to portray with the maximum of intensity—of *life*—those loved objects (stones, hedges, road shapes, dead trees, lezarded rocks) which were at last ready to be brought back from the in-visible, because interior world of stored images. And in doing so he has expressed, as perhaps no other graphic artist has done, that mysteriously ominous or serene, but fundamental movement that I spoke of at the beginning of this essay. Look at the mountain peak in *Black Landscape;* at the fields which clutch the black hill in *Western Hills* like the feet of an insect; at the queer, animal shape of *Gorse on Sea-wall;* at the *Dark Hill* like a moth's wing: here are images of the oneness of Nature, an assertion that the richness and variety of natural forms are bound up with their capacity for imitating each other and—on occasion—Man himself.

It had always seemed to me that, in painting large units of landscape, such as hills, Sutherland had reverted to the practice of the early Flemish and Italian painters and was observing minutely some small object and then magnifying it enormously; so that I was not surprised to read, in the letter I have quoted above, that "I would lie on the warm shore until my eye, becoming riveted to some sea-eroded rocks, would notice that they were precisely repro-ducing, in miniature, the forms of the inland hills."

To see landscape like this is to rediscover the vision of childhood and of primitive man. For what are the gods of primitive peoples—of

Homeric Greece in especial—but the faces that stare suddenly out of the heart of a fire, from the depths of summer leafage, from the outline of a cliff against the sky?—faces that astonish, threaten or comfort in a single flash and then—with a change in the light, or a gust of wind—disappear, leaving a burning log, a green bush, a precipice of stone.

Look at those stooks of corn: they are crouching soldiers. Look again, and they have turned back into quiet piles of folded stalks. Look at that gnarled oak, dead these hundred years: it is a tiger clawing the ground; at the *Metal Container pouring molten iron*: it is a mouth agape in rage. The double image is perfect, complete: these are the gods which surround us.

The moment of ecstasy is always short, but the memory of it does not die. Shelley knew it often, but was usually too impatient to recapture it. Not so Wordsworth: look at Sutherland's *Black Landscape*, or the *Sun Setting Between Hills* and then read the following passage:

A rocky Steep uprose
Above the Cavern of the Willow tree
And now, as suited one who proudly row'd
With his best skill, I fix'd a steady view

Upon the top of that same craggy ridge,
The bound of the horizon; for behind
Was nothing but the stars and the grey sky.
She was an elfin Pinnace; lustily
I dipp'd my oars into the silent Lake,
And, as I rose upon the stroke, my Boat
Went heaving through the water, like a Swan;
When from behind that craggy Steep, till then
The bound of the horizon, a huge Cliff,
As if with voluntary power instinct,
Uprear'd its head. I struck, and struck again,
And, growing still in stature, the huge Cliff
Rose up between me and the stars, and still,
With measur'd motion, like a living thing,
Strode after me. With trembling hands I turn'd
And through the silent water stole my way
Back to the Cavern of the Willow tree.
There in her mooring-place, I left my Bark,
And, through the meadows homeward went,
    with grave
And serious thoughts; and after I had seen
That spectacle, for many days, my brain
Work'd with a dim and undetermin'd sense
Of unknown modes of being; in my thoughts
There was a darkness, call it solitude,
Or blank desertion, no familiar shapes
Of hourly objects, images of trees;

Of sea or sky, no colours of green fields;
But huge and mighty Forms, that do not live
Like living men, mov'd slowly through the mind
By day, and were the trouble of my dreams.

Look now at *Cliff Road* in the light of Shakespeare's

Sometimes we see a cloud that's dragonish;
A vapour sometime like a bear or lion,
A tower'd citadel, a pendant rock,
A forked mountain, or blue promontory
With trees upon't, that nod unto the world
And mock our eyes with air: thou hast seen these
   signs;
They are black vesper's pageants.

And, indeed, in all Sutherland's studies of sunsets, the night cloud is seen sweeping the colours off the landscape as with a big broom.

Look at *Green Tree Form, Red Monolith, Folded Hills*, and then read their equivalents in Gerard Manley Hopkins, in Dylan Thomas and George Barker. Or listen, if you prefer music, to Sibelius' *Tapiola*, in which Nature strikes to kill, or his *Sixth Symphony*, or the Finale of Bartok's *Second String Quartet*. All these works employ that double

imagery which drove Rimbaud away from poetry altogether, lest it destroy him. For to perceive the gods is dangerous, and these visions terrify even while they entrance. A drawing like the *Blasted Oak*, which is a rhapsody of virtuoso penmanship, of bold and varied hatching, makes one feel faint with excess of reality, because in it the artist has discovered the exact point at which Nature herself commits the Pathetic Fallacy—just as Wordsworth and Shakespeare discovered it before him.

For the amateur of these extraordinary pictures, to see a thing is in a sense to become it. One feels oneself enter the landscape; the trees and grasses shoot up round one. It is a mystical sense, as of penetration into a mirror. Hence Graham Sutherland may justly be called a romantic painter, since looking at his pictures induces assent to the proposition: "a landscape is a feeling."

In the choice of media he has experimented freely beyond the usual range, of oil, watercolour, and pen drawing. With water-colour he has achieved some ravishing effects, particularly in the use of washes of black over pink or green. In his oils, in spite of a skilful use of *impasto* and a careful finish to every inch of the canvas, I

13

seem to distinguish a certain heaviness, a lack of fluidity in the pigment which suggests that this is the medium least suited to his purposes. On the whole, I should hazard the suggestion that a combination of chalk and gouache on a basis of ink and water-colour is likely to prove his most useful instrument, since what I should describe as his most successful pictures have been executed in this medium, or some approximation to it.

I cannot leave the subject of Graham Sutherland's art without a reference to the drawings of Henry Moore, for these two are in some sense complementary artists. Between them, that is to say, they create a complete world. Sutherland's forms, in their final state (for he utilizes a series of tiny sketches), are comments on Nature; Moore's drawings display as it were paradigms of the human body. If a figure were to walk into a Sutherland landscape, it could only be one of Henry Moore's cavernous, pin-headed monsters, —skeletons covered, not with flesh, but with a gradual incrustation of stone. There is in these obdurate confederates the same quality of sinister mystery, of wordless plotting, as one finds in— let us say—Sutherland's *Association of Oaks*. Moore's giants are lightly poised on their bases, which are bottle-like or buskined; and if they display features at all, it is a pair of pointed eyes—cruel, because reduced to their lowest terms—or muscles unhooked and hanging loose, like tatters of chiffon, as in those anatomical illustrations of John Stephan of Calcar so much admired by Thomas Lovell Beddoes.

Moore and Sutherland are among those major artists who have had the wits to see that neither man nor his world is naturally *kind*. Even Moore's lead objects teach this lesson: one is afraid to touch them, lest they poison one insidiously, or (alternatively and more probably) go off like mouse-traps and nip one's finger. His figures, both in sculpture and drawing, strike the same note; and so do Graham Sutherland's, now that he has taken to introducing them into his scene. True children of their age, these two artists converge from opposite directions, to meet in the lurid glare of a world of fire and ashes. Moore's are secured in an armour of stone, or swaddled in folds of saturated linen. Sutherland's have little but flesh to protect them; yet with their heroic outlines, wire-drawn by the flare of acetylene on white-hot metal, they are solid and fraternal as their forebears of the high Renaissance.

There are, as I have sought obliquely to indicate, in Moore and Sutherland the materials of a modern mythology. It is not only that, in excellence of technique and invention, they are two of the most significant artists of our time; they possess, as well, the unmoved, receptive eyes which alone can reflect the tragic idyll of contemporary England. The mystery, the intricate beauty—gay with tartan sunbeams or gloomy with undern colour—of Sutherland's landscapes; the aloof and monumental distinction of Moore's beings, grouped against the tunnelled inferno of a world poised between an end and a beginning: here, surely, is a complementary vision that takes us back, in its noble adequacy and completeness, to the stupendous world of Piero della Francesca.

How the art of Graham Sutherland will develop in future I am not competent to predict. Yet his work, since 1940, as a chronicler of England at war, is a pointer. His first essays in a genre foreign to his nature were, I seem to feel, strikingly unsuccessful: his vision was too personal to accommodate itself easily or at once to reporting on lines that the untrained eye could recognize. Then the blitz came, and with it devastation; Sutherland visited bombed Wales (his country of adoption, remember), and quite suddenly he seems to have found his way into a new realm. Drama returned to the landscape, and with it perspective, the visual equivalent of drama. His big devastation pictures of 1940-1 are terrible in their accuracy and ruthless virtuosity: the engineer's apprentice had not learnt his job in vain.

And he has not stopped there. War is nourished by human beings, who had, sooner or later, to come into the picture. They accordingly did so, and the *Tapping a Steel Furnace* became something more than a vivid illustration: it is, I think, one of his finest, as it is certainly one of his most astonishing and original, pictures. The new source of inspiration has continued to flow, and into channels on which the artist was used to draw. In his most recent pictures, of tin stopes and the miners who inhabit them, Sutherland seems at last to have discovered a method of drawing figures of men in terms adequate to their surroundings. His iron workers are faceless —not only because of the visual effect of heat and glare, but because the conditions in which these men work repel, for the time being, the characteristically human expression. Down in the mine it is different. The *mystique* of Nature, which Sutherland has expressed so eloquently in his landscapes, lives again in the inky gloom of these subterranean galleries, and the miners themselves, helmeted and crested with an acetylene flame, look as if they were made of the ore they are engaged in extracting. Yet, unlike the iron workers, each is an individual: their faces and hands are expressed in lines as taut and nervous as Dürer's. These portraits—for that is what they are—are a new point of departure for Sutherland; they represent an ability until now latent in his art. Latent, but always, I think, there: the hand that drew the oak tree in the etching, *Pastoral,* is clearly the same as that which now delineates another kind of worn, hard-bitten feature.

We are back again among the primitive gods: at one moment a knot in oak-bark, at the next a hand emerging from the darkness of a stope; it is the same limb, lit now by the sun, now by a bud of white flame. The double image flickers back and forth: these pictures are all alive, like a wood fire at shut of day, under the ashes. They glow out suddenly, with a wicked gleam, then return to their frames. It has happened to me to return after absence and find them changed (I am thinking especially of *Western Hills,* but others would be the same); a passage here, another there, seems to have increased suddenly in intention, to mean something new in the conjugation of shapes and tones. They alter, too, with the quality and quantity of light they receive, so that at sunset a picture depicting that time of day has more of its quality than by morning light; and vice versa. At night they collect the shadows of the room into themselves. Catching sight of one suddenly in a mirror, as I pass, I know that I am under observation.

Edward Sackville-West

Plate 1 SUN SETTING BETWEEN HILLS. 1938

Plate 2   PASTORAL.   1930

Plate 3   Green Tree Form.   1940

Plate 4   ROAD WITH ROCKS.   1936

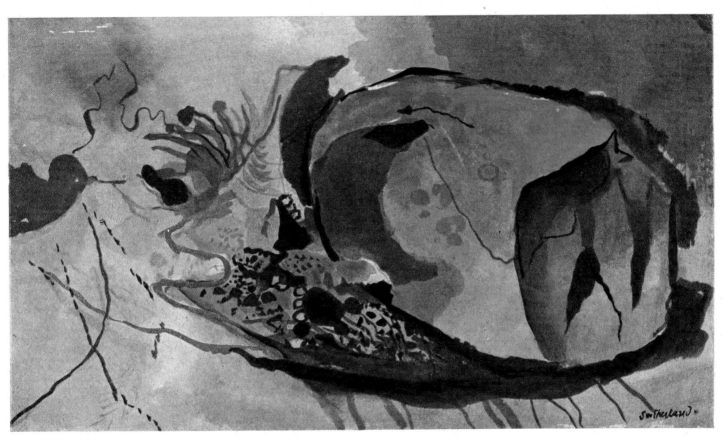

Plate 5   SMALL BOULDER.   1940

Plate 6 TREE TRUNK SPRAWLING. 1938

Plate 7 ENTRANCE TO LANE. 1939

Plate 8 BLACK LANDSCAPE. 1937

Plate 9   RED LANDSCAPE.   1942

Plate 10   ASSOCIATION OF OAKS.   1940

Plate 11 RED MONOLITH. 1937

Plate 12 Precipitous Road to Hills. 1940

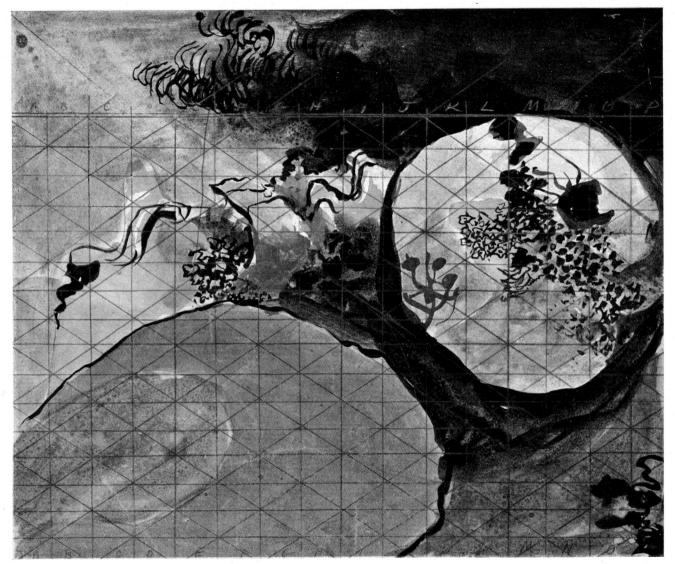

Plate 13   Design for "The Wanderer".   1940

Plate 14 FALLEN TREE AGAINST SUNSET. 1940

G. Sutherland 1939

Plate 15   GORSE ON SEA WALL.   1939

Plate 16   LANDSCAPE WITH LOW CLIFF AND WOODS.   1938

Plate 17   DEVASTATION—House in Wales.   1940

Plate 18   DEVASTATION—City—Burnt-out Interior.   1941

Plate 19   CLIFF ROAD.   1941

Plate 20   WESTERN HILLS.   1938

Plate 21 DEVASTATION—East End Street. 1941

Plate 22   BLASTED OAK.   1941

Plate 23   FURNACES—Slag Ladles.   1942

Plate 24   DEVASTATION—East End—Burnt-out Paper Rolls.   1941

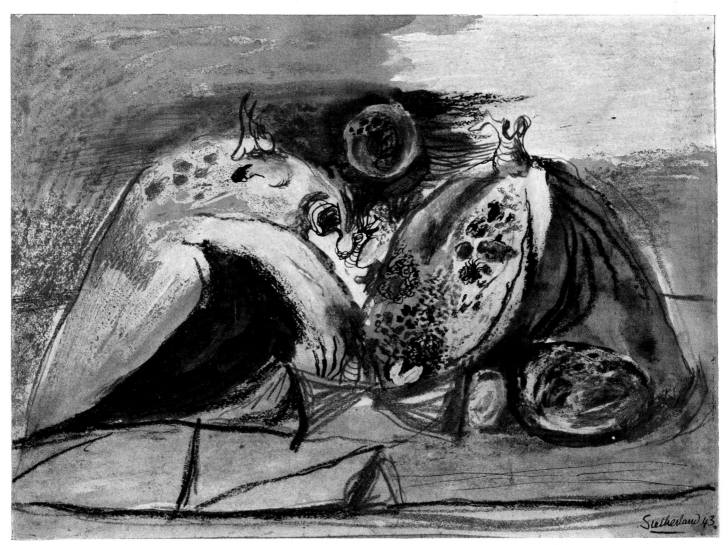

Plate 25 FOLDED HILLS. 1943

Plate 26   DARK HILL.   1940

Plate 27   Devastation—City—Twisted Girders.   1941

Plate 28 TREE FORM. 1941

Plate 29

FURNACES—Tapping a Steel Furnace. 1941

Plate 30 FOLDED HILLS. 1943

Plate 31   TIN MINE—A Declivity.   1942

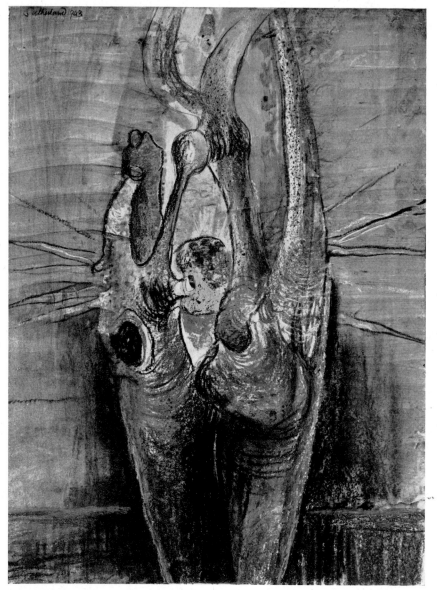

Plate 32 TREE FORMS. 1943